Table of Contents

Introduction and Objectives 1

Setting the Stage for Empowerment 2

Understanding Human Character Strengths 3

Four Steps to Empowerment 4

    I.   **Observe Fears** 5
            Maslow Got It Wrong 6
            Exercise: Preparation Blueprint 9

    II.   **Examine Beliefs** 12
            Exercise: Negative Self-Concept 13
            Exercise: Judgement Spectators 15

    III. **Embrace Risk** 16
            Exercise: Self-Awareness 17
            Exercise: Flipping the Coin 18
            Positive Self Concepts 20
            Positive Emotion list 21
            Turn-Arounds 23

    IV. **Demonstrate Courage** 26
            Character Strengths 27
            Tilt Factors 29
            Commitment Guide 30

Exercise: Energizers and Accountability Partners 32

Exercise: The Arena – What's My Prize? 33

Blueprint 34

Resources 37

INTRODUCTION & OBJECTIVES

Welcome to the Empowerment Strategies Workshop!

Today we will focus on what is fundamental to success in the workplace and in personal development: the ability to face challenges, handle ambiguity, and cultivate courage. Growth requires change, and change involves taking risks and stepping into the unknown. This may not be easy to do. Change is essential for propelling us forward and enabling us to make a positive impact in our world.

> "Only those who dare to fail greatly can ever achieve greatly."
> --Robert F. Kennedy

Why Focus on Empowerment?

In April 1910, 26th President of the United States, Theodore Roosevelt, delivered a speech called "Citizenship in a Republic" at the Sorbonne in Paris, France. Today, it has been cited and used in everything from The New Yorker magazine, to General Motors' Cadillac ads, to a book by Brené Brown called, "True Courage." One of the most famous passages in the speech reads:

"It is not the critic who counts; not the man who points out how the strong man stumbles, or where the doer of deeds could have done them better. The credit belongs to the man who is actually in the arena, whose face is marred by dust and sweat and blood; who strives valiantly; who errs, who comes short again and again, because there is no effort without error and shortcoming; but who does actually strive to do the deeds; who knows great enthusiasms, the great devotions; who spends himself in a worthy cause; who at the best knows in the end the triumph of high achievement, and who at the worst, if he fails, at least fails while True Courage, so that his place shall never be with those cold and timid souls who neither know victory nor defeat."

In this workshop, you'll learn how great leaders rise using courage, resilience, and vulnerability. We will explore how perfectionism, shame, and "the little voices" in our heads can stop us from living the purposeful and fulfilling lives we know we want. Today you will learn the confidence-building tools necessary for daring to take risks, even when the stakes are high.

SETTING THE STAGE

What's the arena event? What's the *prize* to go for? What are those Judgmental Spectators going to yell? The arena is a metaphor for our upcoming fears or stressors (or past, in reflection).

The arena is nerve-racking, risky, and often requires the blood, sweat, and tears of hard work. We are willing to leave the safety and stability of the spectator stands to go for the challenge!

When we go into the arena, it's not just the task that's hard--it's also the self-inflicted negative thinking we hold on to, badgering us while we're there. Our fear of failure, self-doubt (little voices in our head), or the feeling that, no matter what we do, it's never enough, rob us of our journey and the reward.

A prerequisite for engaging in the steps of empowerment will be to first select a particular upcoming stressful situation, then begin using the tools.

Using the theme of "entering the arena," we'll call this particular situation your "event."

Here are some examples:

- Annual performance review meeting (with your manager)
- Stressful group meeting
- Important presentation you must give
- Project deliverable that could impact your career

By the end of this workshop, you'll have a blueprint that both documents your journey into the arena and allows you an opportunity to examine and question your stressful thoughts by offering them a "seat at the table."

We will review extensive research from experts such as researcher, author and public speaker Brené Brown, methodologies from a strengths-based character model called TILT365, and clarity exercises from renowned author and original thought-leader Byron Katie. We highly encourage you to dig deeper into the research of these models and teachers.

UNDERSTANDING HUMAN CHARACTER STRENGTHS

First let's take a step back and look at why humans are so great! From the neuroscience-based Tilt365 model, we can measure character based on four basic human strength meta-factors:

Wisdom	*The ability to collect facts and discern with judgment* Needs: Significance Fears: Inferiority
Humanity	*The ability to live communally and create harmony* Needs: Belonging Fears: Abandonment
Courage	*The ability to take action and seek justice* Needs: Power Fears: Vulnerability
Resilience	*The ability to create new ideas and live with purpose* Needs: Freedom Fears: Constraint

Why is it important to understand this?

Empowerment requires positively influencing others – both in the stands and in the arena.

Question: How do we motivate others, convert naysayers, and achieve our goals?

Answer: Our character.

Based on 20+ years of research (and adopted at companies like Facebook and Redhat), this model shows how your character influences others. The significance of this model is to break down individual character traits so you can understand the needs and fears that make up all personalities. Knowing how to positively influence others at work gains you the support you need to win battles.

These are the four major Character traits. Later, we will be examining these strengths and discovering the ways in which our commitment to them will aid with self-awareness in the arena. During the "Demonstrate Courage" portion of this workshop, we will turn our attention to these influencing traits again to see what happens when they are under-developed, commendable, and overused.

FOUR STEPS TO EMPOWERMENT

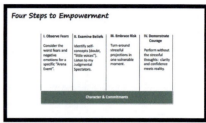

To pursue empowerment, we will move through a progression of steps that address what judgment and fears we hold and how to transform them into courage and resilience by practicing authenticity. We will also look at what truths our fears hold and turn those into catalysts for confidence. Let's start with Observe Fears.

The four key steps we will investigate are:

I. Observe Fears

II. Examine Beliefs

III. Embrace Risk

IV. Demonstrate Courage

I. OBSERVE FEARS:

We'd love to begin our path to Empowerment with nothing but positivity! We love good news, and there's plenty of it if we focus on what we have vs. what we lack. But let's face it: the fact that a situation feels daring means there are fears or stressful thoughts underlying it. So for now, let's go to straight to the heart of what scares of most and is likely holding us back.

Did you know that 72% of people who experience daily stress and anxiety say it interferes with who they truly are? Of course it does – when we are stressed, we may not be acting as our authentic selves.

Because of stress, we are the most in debt, obese, addicted, and medicated adults in U.S. history. Yet, we can't selectively numb emotions. When we numb fears, we numb joy, gratitude, and happiness. We feel miserable because we don't have joy, so we numb again. We blame – what a great way to discharge pain and discomfort: pass the buck. When we passed the buck, did we really feel less stress? We strive for perfection in our bodies, our jobs, and our lives. Can perfection ever truly be achieved?

Here are more statistics:

Job stress has professional and personal consequences.

On the job:
Employees say stress and anxiety most often impacts their …
- workplace performance (56%)
- relationships with coworkers and peers (51%)
- quality of work (50%)
- relationships with superiors (43%)

Personal time:
Over 75% of those who have work stress say it carries into their personal lives.

With spouses and loved ones:
70% of these adults report that workplace stress affects their personal relationships, mainly with their spouses. Though both the majority of men and women report workplace stress as detrimentally affecting their personal relationships, it is statistically more common in men (79%), than women (61%).

The main culprits of work-related stress:
- deadlines (55%)
- interpersonal relationships (53%)
- staff management (50%)
- handling issues/problems that arise (49%)

Source: Anxiety and Depression Association of America

Stress is fear-based and can be attributed to the <u>anxiety of social acceptance.</u> The root of this is fear of exclusion and rejection. Let's explore.

MASLOW GOT IT WRONG

In his theory of motivation, published in 1943, famous and renowned psychologist Abraham Maslow proposed a basic hierarchy, which outlines the individual motivations that drive human beings. Maslow included his observations of humans' innate curiosity, and his theories have been the basis for describing stages of growth in humans for decades. The model describes the pattern through which human motivation generally evolves.

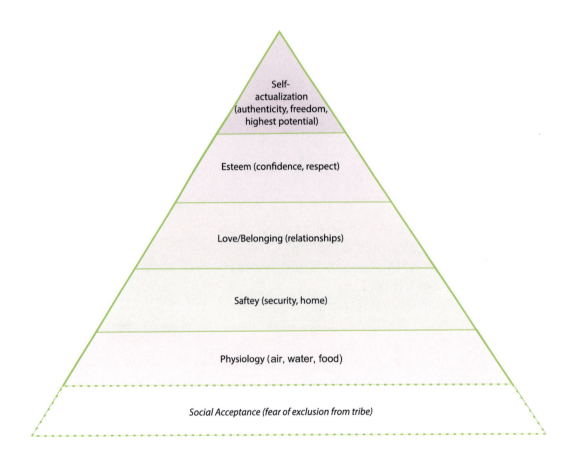

Physiological

Physiological needs are the physical requirements for human survival. If these requirements are not met, the human body cannot function properly and will ultimately fail. These needs are thought to be the most important and should be met first. Maslow suggested air, water, and food as the basic physiological requirements for survival in all animals, including humans.

Safety

When physical needs are relatively satisfied, the individual's safety needs may take precedence and dominate behavior. In the absence of physical safety – due to war, natural disaster, family turmoil/abuse, etc.— people experience internal stresses, disorders, or trauma, and can act out negatively as a result. Economic safety, another subset of this category, may show itself in preferential job status, promotions, or higher salaries. Examples of safety and security needs include:

- personal security
- financial security
- health and well-being
- safety against accidents/illness and their adverse impacts

Love and Belonging

After physiological and safety needs are fulfilled, the third level of human needs is interpersonal and involves feelings of belonging. This need is especially strong in childhood and can override the need for safety, as witnessed in children who cling to abusive parents. Deficiencies within this level of Maslow's hierarchy can impact the individual's ability to form and maintain emotionally significant relationships such as friendships, intimacy, and family/friend connections.

Esteem

All humans have a need to feel respected, and this is directly linked to self-esteem. Low self-esteem may result from imbalances during this level in the hierarchy. For example, people often engage in a profession or hobby to gain recognition, a sense of contribution, or value—but this can be an empty investment. By seeking out fame or glory, sufferers of low self-esteem attempt to gain respect from others; however, self-esteem can only be gained by self-acceptance. Psychological imbalances such as depression can also hinder the person from obtaining a higher level of self-esteem or self-respect.

Self-Actualization

"What a man can be, he must be." The basis of the perceived need for self-actualization includes creativity, spontaneity, problem-solving, lack of prejudice, and acceptance of facts. This level of need refers to what a person's full potential is and the realization of that potential. Maslow believed that to understand this level of need, the person must not only achieve the previous needs, but also master them.

Social Acceptance – What Maslow didn't have on his pyramid

The latest neuroscience-based research suggests that in order to be accepted, people will forfeit food, water, and other levels of needs. With this understanding, everything in Maslow's model rests on a new bottom level: Social Acceptance. Think about how often high school or college kids buckle under peer pressure. The fear of being "voted out of the tribe" is an innate "meta-motivation" described as, "the motivation for people to go beyond their scope of basic needs and strive for something better." Social acceptance drives behaviors, and behaviors drive our ability to succeed much more than we once thought.

> *"Fear of rejection blocks other basic needs, which I would argue is the most powerful motivation there is. The inner-machinery loses its focus and purpose when the need for social acceptance exists."*
> --Roy Baumeister, FSU psychology professor and behavioral research

EXERCISE

PREPARATION BLUEPRINT

Imagine an upcoming (or past) situation that causes stress for you. Is it presenting at an All-Hands meeting? Is it delivering bad news? Is it having a difficult conversation with an important stakeholder? It's important to get the specifics of that situation down, or your mind will take over, running on a full tank of past fears and beliefs. Take your time to think about your trip into the arena.

1. Blueprint: Set the stage.

Describe the event: Title, time, location, topic.
Example: Group communication meeting, next Thurs, 10a, conference area, delivering bad news.

_____

_____

_____

We are born to judge. Everyone does it! This event wouldn't be stressful if someone weren't judging you. We are often our own worst critics, but see if you can exclude yourself from this exercise. Go big, it's all in your head anyway!

2. Blueprint: NOT including yourself, <u>who is potentially judging you the most</u>?

Prioritize your "**Judgmental Spectator**" list.
Example: Priority A. My boss (I want a promotion) B. My co-worker, Pat.

_____

_____

_____

Anything can happen in the arena! You know all the good possibilities, but let's look at the stressful, not-so-good ones. Take your time, search deep inside yourself for your worst fears, memories, projections, and thoughts to get to the specifics of failing.

3. **Blueprint: What's the worst that can happen?**

   Example: I forget my notes, technical issue, voice shakes, someone laughs at me, my zipper is down, my boss cuts me off.

   _____
   _____
   _____

Consider those painful and stressful thoughts and fears. What negative emotions are living for you in that moment? *(See: Negative Emotions List)*

4. **Blueprint: Write down the negative emotions you'd be experiencing:**

   Example: Intimidated, powerless, tortured, embarrassed, uncertain

   _____
   _____
   _____

Now, let's give those fears and emotions a power boost! We want them all to have a seat at the table so we can see them clearly. Within the realm of real possibility, what would make "the worst that can happen" even worse?

5a. **Blueprint: Make it worse! Update your worst-case scenario, and include the behaviors/actions of your Judgmental Spectators.**

   Example: It's now a company-wide meeting, televised live. I'm getting a cold. Pat has been bad-mouthing me to everyone. My update means people will be laid off. My best supporter just quit. My boss's arms are folded, and he's rolling his eyes as he whispers something negative about me to his neighbor.

   _____
   _____
   _____

5b. **Blueprint: Identify if additional negative emotions arise (see list).**

   Example: Terrified, numb, panicked

   _____
   _____
   _____

Negative Emotions List: How do you react when you allow negative thoughts?

Angry	Depressed	Confused	Helpless	Indifferent	Afraid	Hurt	Sad	Judgmental
abrupt	achy	awkward	alone	bored	alarmed	aching	anguished	attacked
aggressive	alienated	blushing	argumentative	cold	anxious	afflicted	blindsided	blunt
agitated	ashamed	comparing	authoritative	agonized	apprehensive	crying	bossy
annoyed	bad	compulsive	condescending	dull	attached	appalled	desolate	brutal
antagonistic	blocked	condescending	confounded	insensitive	attacking	belittled	devastated	combative
bitter	bummed out	craving	demanding	lifeless	avoiding	bulldozed	dirty	complaining
condemning	burdened	cut off	disdainful	preoccupied	bullied	disconnected	disgusted
contrary	cheerless	disillusioned	reserved	cowardly	crushed	discontented	fake
controlling	closed	distrustful	disdainful	robotic	defensive	deprived	dismayed	frowning
critical	contracted	doubtful	dishonest	slow	disrupted	disturbed	downhearted	glaring
cross	crabby	embarrassed	distracted	sluggish	dreadful	distant	fragile	hard
disrespectful	cranky	distressed	distraught	tired	fearful	heartbroken	grieved	hurtful
enraged	dejected	doomed	uncaring	frightened	humiliated	groaning	neglectful
envious	denigrating	empty	uninterested	guarded	indignant	lonely	obsessive
exasperated	despairing	fatigued	out of sorts	unresponsive	immobile	injured	moaning	phony
frustrated	desperate	fidgety	pessimistic	weary	inhibited	insulted	mournful	pushy
furious	despicable	frenzied	powerless		invaded	miffed	oversensitive	ranting
hateful	despondent	hesitant	punishing		insecure	offended	remorseful	recoiling
hitting	diminished	hungry	resistant		intimidated	pained	self-	rude
hostile	disappointed	indecisive	rotten		intolerant	rejected	castigating	scolding
hotheaded	discouraged	jittery	nauseated		menaced	secretive	sorrowful	serious
impatient	disheartened	lost	perplexed		nervous	slighted	sour	shallow
incensed	dissatisfied	misgiving	shy		panicked	smothered	sullen	shrill
infuriated	down	incapable	sick		paranoid	suffering	tearful	stern
insulting	drawn	incapacitated	squirming		petrified	tormented	unhappy	stiff
insulting	faultfinding	incompetent	stressed		phobic	tortured	unworthy	stilted
irate	gloomy	inept	tense		prejudiced	victimized		stonewalling
irritated	glum	inferior	trapped		restless	withdrawn		stony
jealous	grouchy	judgmental	trembling		rigid	wronged		tactless
loud	grumpy	manipulative	twitching		scared			taut
mad		off-kilter	uncertain		self-absorbed			territorial
malicious		overwhelmed	uncomfortable		self-conscious			unfair
mean		paralyzed	uneasy		shaky			
mean-spirited		pathetic	unsure		suspicious			
offensive		shut	useless		terrified			
overbearing		superior	vulnerable		threatened			
poisonous		weak			timid			
quarrelsome		woozy			troubled			
reactive					unbending			
rebellious					unwelcoming			
reprimanding					uptight			
repulsed					wary			
resentful					worried			
retaliating								
revengeful								
sadistic								
sarcastic								
scornful								
screaming								
seething								
sharp								
short-tempered								
spiteful								
stubborn								
swearing								
ticked off								
unpleasant								
upset								
venomous								
vindictive								
violent								
yelling								

EMPOWERMENT STEPS (continued)

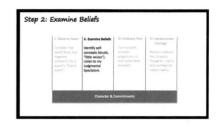

Now we are ready to go on to the next step.

  I. Observe Fears

  II. Examine Beliefs

  III. Embrace Risk

  IV. Demonstrate Courage

II. EXAMINE BELIEFS & STORIES

EXERCISE

NEGATIVE SELF-CONCEPT

Let's look at stories that are created and fed by our fears. These beliefs and stories create a negative self-concept.

Common negative thoughts stem from comparing ourselves to others, feeling that we don't have enough, and a desire to be perfect and have no shame.

Perfectionism is a self-destructive and addictive belief system that fuels this primary thought: If I do everything perfectly, I can avoid or minimize the painful feelings of shame, judgment, and blame. Perfectionism is self-destructive simply because perfection doesn't exist. It's an unattainable, abusive goal.

6a. Blueprint: Self-Concepts – Perfection
In your situation, why (if at all) aren't you perfect?

I am/I am not:
Example: I am not the best. I am not doing it right.

_____

_____

_____

Shame is a universal and primitive experience. It is the intensely painful feeling or experience of believing that we are flawed and therefore unworthy of love and belonging. Categories where shame exists include: physical appearance, intelligence level, emotions (crying/anger), money/wealth, job title/function, and general stereotypes/labels.

6b. Blueprint: Self-Concepts – Shame
In your situation, where could shame exist within you?

I am/I am not:
Example: I am not financially successful. I am not at the job title I should be..

_____

_____

_____

"If you compare, you will always lose." Rarely do we compare ourselves to people whom we think we've surpassed in some way. Our search for acceptance has us constantly on the lookout for someone with a better home, better job, better car, etc., and once we've found them, we start in with abusive self-talk and shame. It's a losing proposition.

6c. Blueprint: Self-Concepts – Comparing
When you compare yourself to others, what do you conclude?

I am/I am not:
Example: I am not as successful as Pat. I am not as quick on my feet as Pat.

_____
_____
_____

A common vicious circle is making achievements but never feeling that they, or we, are enough. Advertisements, colleagues, movies, and "Facebook-likes" show status and wealth, which can set us up for comparing and then rob us of the joy of accomplishment. "Never enough" thoughts include:

"I got a new apartment."	→	*"It's still not a house."*
"I just got a car."	→	*"It's not that great of a car."*
"I got a promotion."	→	*"But I should be further in my career."*

6d. Blueprint: Self-Concepts – Never Enough
In your situation, where do you believe you're not enough?

I am/I am not:
Example: I am not financially good enough. I am not funny enough.

_____
_____
_____

6e. Blueprint: Self-Concepts – Negative "Little Voices"
What other beliefs or stories do you tell yourself regularly (those "little voices") that are not positive, are abusive, or nag at you and your spirit?

I am/I am not:
Example: I am a failure. I am incapable of pleasing my parents.

_____
_____
_____

JUDGMENTAL SPECTATORS:

Now look at your Judgmental Spectator **(Question #2)** when you're feeling all these specific negative emotions.

7a. Blueprint: What do you <u>want</u> from your Judgmental Spectators?
   What advice do you have for them?

   I want:
   Example: My boss not to sneer. I want my boss's approval.

   _____
   _____
   _____

7b. Blueprint: What do you <u>need</u> from your Judgmental Spectators?

   They should/shouldn't:
   Example: They should be supportive. They shouldn't bad-mouth me.

   _____
   _____
   _____

8. Blueprint: What is the worst impression or worst experience that you fear you'll have?

   I don't ever want:
   Example: To look stupid. To feel unappreciated.

   _____
   _____
   _____

> "Only those who will risk going too far can possibly find out how far one can go."
> --T.S. Eliot

EMPOWERMENT STEPS (continued)

Now we are ready to go on to the next step.

    I. Observe Fears

    II. Examine Beliefs

    III. Embrace Risk

    IV. Demonstrate Courage

III. EMBRACE RISK

Nice work! Now, let's start to understand how our fears and beliefs can be evaluated. What if those fears and beliefs were exposed in an effective way?

We'll now investigate <u>truths and myths that you may be holding</u>.
We will look at vulnerability and turning-around the fears we are potentially projecting.

A few dictionary definitions of vulnerability include:

- Vulnerability is the state of being open to injury, or appearing as if you are.
- Vulnerability might be emotional, like admitting that you're in love with someone who might only like you as a friend.
- Vulnerability is being in a position where others may cause damage or harm to you.

If we investigate the theory, "Vulnerability lies someplace between courage and fear" (Brené Brown), we must also understand what is real for us, as pertains to Vulnerability. Please answer these questions for yourself, and then we will share observations with a partner.

EXERCISE

SELF-AWARENESS: What is Vulnerability to you?

How do you define vulnerability? How does it feel to you?
_____
_____
_____

How was vulnerability viewed while you were growing up? How was it viewed in school?
_____
_____
_____

What physical sensations arise in your body (tightness, heart rate, headache) when you are most vulnerable?
_____
_____
_____

EXERCISE

FLIPPING THE COIN

> **Debunking Myths**
>
> #1: Vulnerability is a Weakness
>
> #2: Vulnerability and Work Don't Mix
>
> What Else Comes to Mind?

Let's look at some common myths on Vulnerability and share what we know from our personal experiences. We'll use an exercise called *Flipping the Coin,* which involves looking at each myth and investigating the opposite perspective. Pay attention to what rings true for you as we look more deeply into debunking the common myths of Vulnerability.

As we've seen, some people view vulnerability as a strength. Others say it is a weakness, a threat to acceptance, and a way to promote negative judgments from others.

Can you remember watching someone express vulnerability in public? What was the example, and how did you view them?

Debunking Myth #1: Vulnerability Is a Weakness

_____
_____
_____
_____
_____
_____

Below is a list of commonly mentioned statements that <u>may show vulnerability at work</u>. Can you find real-world examples to debunk the myth: Vulnerability and work don't mix?

"I don't know." *"I need help."*

"I'd like to try doing that!" *"I disagree, can we discuss?"*

"I risked a lot and failed." *"Here's what I learned."*

"Here's what I really need." *"I'd like some feedback."*

"Can I get your honest opinion?" *"How can I improve going forward?"*

"I played a part in that." *"I accept total responsibility."*

"I'm here for you." *"How can I support you?"*

"Let's forget about the past." *"That means a lot to me"*

"I messed up; I'm sorry." *"Thank you for letting me try this."*

Debunking Myth #2: Vulnerability and Work Don't Mix

_____
_____
_____
_____
_____
_____

> "Truth and courage aren't always comfortable, but they're never a weakness."
> --Brené Brown

EXERCISE

POSITIVE SELF-CONCEPT

When you look at the Negative Emotions List, it's a prescription for pain. Choosing to allow ourselves to be vulnerable to our emotions puts us in the position to transition into positive thinking. Using the tools from the "Flipping the Coin" exercise, lets flip our Negative Self-Concepts from **Question #6**. In this case, we allow ourselves to be vulnerable and acknowledge our fears but are willing to enter the arena with a Positive Self-Concept.

In baseball, imagine a batter walking up to home plate. The score is tied, the bases are loaded, there are two outs, it's full-count, and the pitcher throws what looks to be a good pitch. If he were carrying a helmet full of negative emotions like "terrified" and "paralyzed," who would that batter be? How would he show up? Most batters would tell you they wouldn't have as much confidence or luck.

What if the batter showed up with positive emotions like "focused" and "confident"—who do you think would have better odds of winning the game?

Go back and look at your Negative Self-Concepts. Who would you be in the arena without those negative thoughts? How would you act? Authentic? Confident, because I will only do my best in that moment, and won't be able to change the outcome? Look at the Positive Emotions list for ideas!

9. **Blueprint: Positive Self-Concept**

    Look at the Positive Emotions List, and identify who you would be without those fears, stressful thoughts, beliefs, and stories.

    _____
    _____
    _____

"It's not the Arena that causes our suffering, it's believing negative thoughts before we arrive."
--*Simplified Coach*

Positive Emotions List: Who would you be without negative thoughts?

Open	Loving	Happy	Interested	Alive	Positive	Peaceful	Strong	Relaxed
accepting	admiring	blissful	absorbed	active	adaptable	adequate	complete	aware
approachable	affectionate	cheerful	amazed	animated	approving	assured	composed	beaming
confident	allowing	child-like	amused	communicative	beautiful	at ease	dynamic	centered
connected	appreciative	delighted	attentive	courageous	bold	authentic	energized	efficient
easy	attracted	easygoing	courteous	energetic	brave	balanced	excellent	fluid
embracing	caring	ecstatic	curious	enjoying	conscientious	blessed	hardy	glowing
empathetic	close	elated	engrossed	equal	constructive	bright	honest	graceful
flexible	compassionate	euphoric	fascinated	excited	cooperative	calm	mature	grounded
flowing	considerate	festive	focused	exhilarated	creative	carefree	perseverant	healthy
free	devoted	fun-loving	inquisitive	frisky	daring	certain	reliable	laughing
friendly	expansive	glad	intent	funny	eager	clear	responsible	light
harmonious	gentle	gleeful	intrigued	giving	earnest	comfortable	sane	meditative
interested	gracious	glorious	involved	great	enthusiastic	confident	secure	natural
kind	grateful	gratified	observant	intelligent	exuberant	content	self-affirming	non-controlling
listening	honoring	happy-go-lucky	thoughtful	liberated	helpful	encouraged	solid	open-minded
outgoing	humble	in good humor		optimistic	honored	fine	stable	placid
present	kindly	in heaven		playful	hopeful	forgiving	supportive	radiant
receptive	loved	innocent		sharing	in the zone	fulfilled	sure	reflective
satisfied	nonjudgmental	jovial		spirited	inspired	genuine	tenacious	rested
sympathetic	passionate	joyous		spunky	keen	good	truthful	smiling
tolerant	patient	jubilant		thrilled	motivated	grateful	unique	spontaneous
understanding	respectful	lighthearted		tickled	privileged	okay		steady
welcoming	sensitive	mellow		vigorous	productive	pleased		still
	sweet	on top of the world		wonderful	resourceful	quiet		supported
	tender	overjoyed		youthful	responsive	relaxed		trusting
	touched	rapturous			upbeat	self-sufficient		unassuming
	warm	satisfied				serene		unhurried
		sunny				sincere		waiting
		thankful				surprised		
						unburdened		
						uplifted		

TURN-AROUNDS AND EMBRACE FEARS

Now we've got all the worries, fears, and myths out on the table. The amazing work of Byron Katie shows us how we project our past pain and suffering onto the people who come into our lives. By turning a statement around, we can see where we can offer ourselves advice and compassion. Each turn-around is an opportunity to experience the opposite of the original statement.

Most people say they are not doing their best work when they are under stress. The baseball batter who shows up to the plate with tied score and bases loaded can hold negative emotions (fear) or positive emotions (motivation). The goal is to consider how the opposite of the original thought can bring truth and peace.

For example, look back at your answers to **Question #7,** and turn each statement around. Identify 2-3 examples of how that new statement could be true for you. You'll be surprised how often you can give yourself what you really want! We'll turn around the examples so you'll get the hang of it:

I want:

>*My boss to stop sneering at me. Their approval.*
>*Their recognition for how hard I'm working.*

Turn-arounds:

>*I want to stop sneering at myself. (How is that true for you?)*
>>*I'm always making disparaging comments to myself!*
>
>*I want my own approval.*
>>*I'm the only one whose approval can ever truly matter.*
>
>*I want recognition from myself for how hard I'm working.*
>>*I am working as hard as I am capable. I could always work harder, but my body and mind let me know when I need a break, and I should thank them for it, considering how hard I push them.*

They should/shouldn't:

> *Shouldn't be so judgmental. Shouldn't bad-mouth me. Should be compassionate. Should tell me I'm doing a great job.*

Turn-arounds:

> *I shouldn't be so judgmental of myself. (How is that true for you?)*
> > *I sound like my parents, and I didn't like it then either.*
>
> *I shouldn't bad-mouth myself.*
> > *I constantly say bad things about myself.*
>
> *I should be compassionate toward myself.*
> > *I should feel good when I leave work with things still to do. I put in the best day that I could, and I should accept that with kindness.*
>
> *I should tell myself I'm doing a great job.*
> > *I'd love some positive feedback, and I'm the only one who truly can know if I mean it!*

10. Blueprint:

Look back at your **Question #7a** and **Question #7b** statement under Judgmental Spectators. Turn-around these statements by swapping pronouns between "them" and "I." See if there is any truth to the turn-around.

I want (Original):
Example: I want my boss not to sneer. I want my boss's approval.

Turn-arounds (New):
Example: He's allowed to have his opinion. I'm doing my best. It's all I can do.

_____

_____

They should/shouldn't (Original):
Example: Shouldn't be so judgmental.

Turn-arounds (New):
Example: I shouldn't be so judgmental of myself.

_____

_____

Now, let's turn around your answers to **Question #8**, then add a preamble of:

"I am willing to..." or *"I look forward to..."*

This turn-around is about embracing all of life <u>without fear and being open to reality.</u> If your boss never compliments you even though you've asked for it, that's reality. Arguing with reality causes more stress. If you look forward to not receiving any compliments because you understand that as the reality of your situation, those thoughts will go from looking like a venomous snake to a piece of rope—harmless.

Uncomfortable feelings are clear reminders that we're attached to something that just may not be true, or reality.

It is also important to note that not everybody is ready or welcoming of this responsibility. If you are not ready for this level of commitment, it's okay. Sometimes the timing is not right due to other circumstances in our lives. Use this time to plan for the process once you are ready.

For example, if you completely fumble a speech, you'll have fresh data to consider:
1) You've learned that you didn't prepare enough because of circumstances.
2) You had a bad day!
3) This isn't the right job for you?

See how these turn-arounds can <u>show your vulnerability and power</u>. Find how each statement is true for you!

NOW EMBRACE YOUR FEARS!

Original Statement examples: To look stupid. To see people whispering. To feel judged. To not look good. To have my status affected. To not feel appreciated.

"I am willing to/I look forward to…"

*I am willing to look stupid. (How is that true for you?)
   I'll do my best. That's all I can ever do.*

*I look forward to seeing people whispering.
   It's likely not about me anyway!*

I am willing to feel judged. (Everyone does it.)

I am willing to not look good.

I look forward to having my status affected.

I am willing to not feel appreciated.

11. Blueprint: Embrace Fears

Look at your answer to **Question #3**, what you don't ever want to experience again in this situation.
I don't ever want:

_____

_____

_____

"Vulnerability: The willingness to share our inner thoughts, hopes, fears, and dreams."
   --Simplified Coach

EMPOWERMENT STEPS (continued):

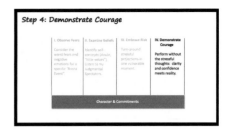

Now we are ready to go on to the next step.

    I. Observe Fears

    II. Examine Beliefs

    III. Embrace Risk

    IV. Demonstrate Courage

IV. DEMONSTRATE COURAGE

Character Strengths

People will access, underuse, or overuse their strengths when entering a challenging or vulnerable state, such as the arena.

Remember when we referred earlier to the Human Strengths, or Character In The Arena Needs? They are separated into four categories.

It's time to look at our Character in the Arena:

<u>Wisdom</u>: *the ability to collect facts and discern with judgment*

    Strengths:
- Perspective
- Focus
- Diligence

<u>Humanity</u>: *the ability to live communally and create harmony*

    Strengths:
- Trust
- Consideration
- Likability

<u>Courage</u>: *the ability to take action and seek justice*

    Strengths:
- Confidence
- Boldness
- Integrity

<u>Resilience</u>: *the ability to create new ideas and live with purpose*

    Strengths:
- Openness
- Inspiration
- Creativity

"Belonging doesn't require us to change who we are; it requires us to be who we are."
--*Brené Brown*

We love lists that inspire your thinking as you prepare for the arena! Let's investigate:

- Underdeveloped Traits
- Commendable Traits
- Overused Traits

Now, let's look at how we *want* to show up at work, in the arena, or in the world. What traits on the Tilt Factors list ring most true for you when you are at your very best performance level? What will you want to consider, or get mentoring on?

12. Blueprint: Commendable, Underdeveloped, and Overused Strengths

What are your underdeveloped traits?

_____

What are you commendable traits?

_____

What are your overused traits?

_____

Take a look at the strengths traits as you envision yourself in the arena. Where do you want to have awareness? Anything you want to consider?

_____
_____
_____

TILT FACTORS

THE 4 META FACTORS

	CORE LEADERSHIP STRENGTHS	Under-Developed Traits	Commendable Traits	Over-Used Traits
WISDOM: HEAD — JUDGMENT ▶ TRUTH	**PERSPECTIVE** Practices Good Judgment	Illogical Subjective Irrational Unrealistic	Logical Objective Rational Realistic	Robotic Scrutinizing Skeptical Paranoid
	FOCUS Attends to Priorities	Aimless Scattered Unselective Undiscerning	Purposeful Mindful Selective Discerning	Intolerant Stoic Particular Critical
	DILIGENCE Effective at Execution	Unproductive Undisciplined Inconsistent Indifferent	Productive Disciplined Consistent Conscientious	Workaholic Obsessive Rigid Meticulous
HUMANITY: HEART — PEOPLE ▶ HARMONY	**LIKABILITY** Expands Social Influence	Unapproachable Unappreciative Stingy Humorless	Approachable Appreciative Generous Humorous	Complient Flattering Indulgent Sarcastic
	CONSIDERATION Thoughtful About Impact	Uncompassionate Rejecting Irreverent Blaming	Compassionate Accepting Respectful Forgiving	Permissive Indifferent Lenient Tolerant
	TRUST Builds Strong Relationships	Boastful Restless Superficial Fickle	Humble Patient Authentic Reliable	Self-Minimizing Compliant Revealing Subservient
COURAGE: GUT — ACTION ▶ JUSTICE	**CONFIDENCE** Exudes a Commanding Presence	Insecure Indecisive Uncertain Passive	Self-Assured Decisive Certain Assertive	Arrogant Dismissive Defensive Aggressive
	BOLDNESS Willing to Face Risk	Timid Cautious Apathetic Resigned	Brave Adventurous Passionate Tenacious	Reckless Rebellious Antagonistic Stubborn
	INTEGRITY Serves as a Good Example	Secretive Unfair Unethical Political	Honest Fair Ethical Honorable	Blunt Righteous Strict Judgmental
RESILIENCE: SPIRIT — IDEAS ▶ PURPOSE	**OPENNESS** Insatiable Curiosity for learning	Unreceptive Complacent Inflexible Inattentive	Receptive Curious Agile Alert	Chaotic Intrusive Erratic Impulsive
	INSPIRATION Casts a Compelling Vision	Withdrawn Mundane Apathetic Pessimistic	Visionary Compelling Enthusiastic Optimistic	Grandiose Overzealous Anxious Idealistic
	CREATIVITY Designs Inventive Solutions	Uninventive Calculated Unimaginative Dependent	Ingenious Intuitive Innovative Resourceful	Eccentric Opinionated Opportunistic Mischevious

COMMITMENTS GUIDE
Acting with Purpose

Commitments are like mantras from which specific actions may be identified. Commitments are first to myself, then to my team or others around me. <u>Use this as a reference guide to create or refine your commitments.</u>

Resilience: Be Unique. Have Compelling Basis for Change.

Openness:
- \+ I commit to being open to continuous learning from everyone.
- \- *(I commit to being right and closed to learning.)*

Inspiration:
- \+ I commit to living in the world of possibility where my creativity soars.
- \- *(I commit to keep doing what continually saps my energy.)*

Creativity:
- \+ I commit to generating novel work that expresses my purpose.
- \- *(I commit to being what others want me to be.)*

Courage: Be Bold. Have Respect.

Integrity:
- \+ I commit to keeping impeccable agreements.
- \- *(I commit to keeping commitments only when it's convenient.)*

Boldness:
- \+ I commit to taking risks to overcome fears or take on new challenges.
- \- *(I commit to playing it safe.)*

Confidence:
- \+ I commit to being honest about my convictions.
- \- *(I commit to concealing my true convictions.)*

Wisdom: Be Wise. Have Credibility.

Perspective:
- \+ I commit to investigating the various ways to see the facts.
- \- *(I commit to positioning the facts in a way that serves what I want.)*

Focus:
- \+ I commit to being mindful about what is important to me.
- \- *(I commit to letting my mind wander wherever it goes.)*

Diligence:
- \+ I commit to being disciplined about my responsibilities.
- \- *(I commit to being lazy about attending to my responsibilities.)*

Humanity: Be Kind. Have Positive Relationships.

Trust:
- \+ I commit to being reliable – with myself, my team, and others.
- \- *(I commit to being unreliable -- with myself, my team, and others.)*

Consideration:
- \+ I commit to being compassionate toward myself, my team, and others.
- \- *(I commit to being insensitive toward myself, my team, and others.)*

Likability:
- \+ I commit to being lighthearted toward myself, my team, and others.
- \- *(I commit to being harsh/judgmental toward myself, my team, and others.)*

COMMITMENTS

Now that you can see a path to Empowerment, what commitments would you like to consider? Commitments let you look at your strengths and create mantras from which specific actions may be identified. Commitments are first to yourself, then to your team or others around you. Refer to the Commitments Guide while considering your trip to the arena.

13. **Blueprint: Commitments**

    With our Character comes a guide, which we can leverage to question whether we are acting with purpose. Review this guide as you think of your situation.

    What commitments do you want to honor most for yourself and others while in the arena?

    _____
    _____
    _____

> "Vulnerability is the birthplace of love, belonging, joy, courage, empathy, accountability, and **authenticity**."
> –Brené Brown

EXERCISE

ENERGIZERS AND ACCOUNTABILITY PARTNER(S)

Let's experiment with providing jeers and cheers to a willing party in each group. Take a moment to decide who will go first to present a daring new idea. The rest of the group will begin with stating nothing but jeers, about every 10 seconds. Debrief. Then the group will express cheers every 10 seconds or so. Debrief. What happens when you receive cheers and jeers? What happens when you give cheers and jeers? Knowing that there will always be negative spectators in the audience, consider allowing them their thoughts, because everyone is judgmental. Consider how not to take these jeers personally, which can interrupt your success in the arena.

What did you notice?

_____
_____
_____

Energizers

Energizers are people who advocate for you or your team, have your back, believe in you, and support and energize you! They may be a member of your team or not. You may want to specifically ask them to offer the kinds of cheers you'd like to hear from them while you're in the arena! Who are your energizers in this situation?

Accountability Partners

Accountability partners will help you keep your specific commitments in the arena. They want you to succeed! Remember the Strengths Traits checklist and Commitments Guide? Work with your Accountability Partner to better understand your range—where you're strong and where you'll need to avoid traits that can derail you. Ask them for any counsel they think may be helpful.

Take the opportunity to "get Vulnerable" with your Accountability Partner and ask for what you need!

An Attitude of Gratitude

Your cheering section will offer time and energy to see you succeed (even if that means you failed!) It's always a good idea to offer them feedback when you leave the arena. What could you say/do to offer gratitude to them? List and describe.

14. Blueprint: Energizers and Accountability Partners

> My Energizers:
>
> My Accountability Partner(s):
>
> How I will show gratitude:

EXERCISE

THE ARENA - WHAT'S MY PRIZE?

You are there – you can see it! What's your real prize in the arena? Some say they "hit it out of the park." Some say, "I'm proud of myself, no matter what." Some say, "I have clarity and confidence that I prepared, and the rest is simply reality."

15. Blueprint: The Arena: What's my Prize?

_____

_____

CREATING YOUR OWN EMPOWERMENT BLUEPRINT

The process of Empowerment is about giving yourself the freedom to be authentic, <u>who you are,</u> and contributing to the world in the most authentic way possible.

Now you have a tool, a blueprint, to make your trip to the arena a success, no matter what. (There are no mistakes, there's only reality!)

Before you enter your next arena—whether it's a challenging conversation, a televised presentation, or anything else that makes you feel you're Empowered —you'll have a blueprint to guide you. You can Observe Fears, Examine Beliefs, Embrace Risk, and Demonstrate Courage – you'll have a plan.

Go, get after it!

> "Vulnerability sounds like truth and feels like courage."
> —Brené Brown

True Courage Arena: Preparation Blueprint

Observe Fears

Arena Event

1. Describe the event: title, time, location, topic.
   Example: Comm Meeting, Thurs 10a, conf area.

2. List Judgmental Spectators
   Example: My boss (I want a promotion). My coworker, Pat.

Worst That Can Happen

3. What's the worst that can happen?
   Example: Forget my notes, voice shakes, technical issues, boss cuts me off.

4. What negative emotions are you feeling?
   Example: Intimidated, powerless, tortured, uncertain. (See Negative Emotions List)

Now Make It Even Worse

5a. Amplify/expand on #3.
   Example: Now the entire company is attending.

5b. Amplify/expand on #4.
   Example: Terrified, paralyzed with fear.

Examine Beliefs

Negative Self-Concept

6a-e. Perfectionism, shame, comparing, never feeling good enough, "little voices" in your head.
   Example: I'm not smart enough.
   I am/I am not:
   I am not as successful as Pat.

Judgmental Spectators

7a. How do you want them to change; what do you want them to do?
   Example: I don't want my boss to sneer.
   I want:

7b. What advice do you have for them?
   Example: They shouldn't bad-mouth me.
   They should/shouldn't:

Worst Impression

8. What is the worst impression or experience that you fear you'll have?
   Example: I don't want to feel unappreciated.

Embrace Risk

Positive Self-Concept

9. Who would I be without ever having these thoughts? (See Positive Emotions List)

Turn-Arounds

10. What is the turn-around? How is it true for you?
    Example: I did my best. He's allowed an opinion.
    Response: *I may be imagining that he's sneering.*

    Example: They should bad-mouth me.
    Response: *They're allowed to gossip. I do it, too. I am confident in my work.*

Embrace Fears

11. I am willing to/I look forward to (worst case): How would this outcome be alright?
    Example: I look forward to feeling unappreciated.
    Response: *I did my best. I can't control their thoughts.*

Demonstrate Courage

Character Strengths

12. Awareness in your Event #1: (See Tilt-Factors list)
    Underdeveloped:
    Commendable:
    Overused:

Commitments

13. What do you want to honor for yourself and others in the arena? (See Commitments Guide)

Energizers and Accountability

14. My Energizers:
    My Accountability Partner(s):
    How I will show gratitude:

The Arena

15. What's my prize?
    Example: I reward myself for bravery regardless of outcome.

True Courage Arena: Preparation Blueprint

Observe Fears

Arena Event

1. Describe the event: title, time, location, topic.
Example: Comm Meeting, Thurs 10a, conf area.

2. List Judgmental Spectators
Example: My boss (I want a promotion), My coworker, Pat.

Worst That Can Happen

3. What's the worst that can happen?
Example: Forget my notes, voice shakes, technical issues, boss cuts me off.

4. What negative emotions are you feeling?
Example: Intimidated, powerless, tortured, uncertain. (See Negative Emotions List)

Now Make It Even Worse

5a. Amplify/expand on #3.
Example: Now the entire company is attending.

5b. Amplify/expand on #4.
Example: Terrified, paralyzed with fear.

Examine Beliefs

Negative Self-Concept

6a-e. Perfectionism, shame, comparing, never feeling good enough, "little voices" in your head.
Example: I'm not as successful as Pat.

I am/I am not:

Judgmental Spectators

7a. How do you want them to change; what do you want them to do?
Example: I don't want my boss to sneer.

I want:

7b. What advice do you have for them?
Example: They shouldn't bad-mouth me.

They should/shouldn't:

Worst Impression

8. What is the worst impression or experience that you fear you'll have?
Example: I don't want to feel unappreciated.

Embrace Risk

Positive Self-Concept

9. Who would I be without ever having these thoughts? (See Positive Emotions List)

Turn-Arounds

10. What is the turn-around? How is it true for you?
Example: I want my boss to sneer.
Response: I did my best. He's allowed an opinion. I may be imagining that he's sneering.

Example: They should bad-mouth me.
Response: They're allowed to gossip. I do it, too. I am confident in my work.

Embrace Fears

11. I am willing to/I look forward to (worst case): How would this outcome be alright?
Example: I look forward to feeling unappreciated.
Response: I did my best. I can't control their thoughts.

Demonstrate Courage

Character Strengths

12. Awareness in your Event #1: (See Tilt-Factors list)
Underdeveloped:

Commendable:

Overused:

Commitments

13. What do you want to honor for yourself and others in the arena? (See Commitments Guide)

Energizers and Accountability

14. My Energizers:

My Accountability Partner(s):

How I will show gratitude:

The Arena

15. What's my prize?
Example: I reward myself for bravery regardless of outcome.

True Courage Arena: Preparation Blueprint

Observe Fears

Arena Event
1. Describe the event: title, time, location, topic.
Example: *Comm Meeting. Thurs 10a, conf area.*

Judgmental Spectators
2. List Judgmental Spectators
Example: *My boss (I want a promotion). My coworker, Pat.*

Worst That Can Happen
3. What's the worst that can happen?
Example: *Forget my notes, voice shakes, technical issues, boss cuts me off.*

Now Make It Even Worse
4. What negative emotions are you feeling?
Example: *Intimidated, powerless, tortured, uncertain.* (See Negative Emotions List)

5a. Amplify/expand on **#3**.
Example: *Now the entire company is attending.*

5b. Amplify/expand on **#4**.
Example: *Terrified, paralyzed with fear.*

Examine Beliefs

Negative Self-Concept
6a-e. Perfectionism, shame, comparing, never feeling good enough, "little voices" in your head.
Example: *I'm not as successful as Pat.*

I am/I am not:
I am not as successful as Pat.

Judgmental Spectators
7a. How do you want them to change; what do you want them to do?
Example: *I don't want my boss to sneer.*

I want:

7b. What advice do you have for them?
Example: *They shouldn't bad-mouth me.*

They should/shouldn't:

Worst Impression
8. What is the worst impression or experience that you fear you'll have?
Example: *I don't want to feel unappreciated.*

Embrace Risk

Positive Self-Concept
9. Who would I be without ever having these thoughts? (See Positive Emotions List)

Turn-Arounds
10. What is the turn-around? How is it true for you?
Response: *I did my best. He's allowed an opinion. I may be imagining that he's sneering.*

Example: *They* **should** *bad-mouth me.*
Response: *They're allowed to gossip. I do it, too. I am confident in my work.*

Embrace Fears
11. I am willing to/I look forward to (worst case): How would this outcome be alright?
Example: *I look forward to feeling unappreciated.*
Response: *I did my best. I can't control their thoughts.*

Demonstrate Courage

Character Strengths
12. Awareness in your Event **#:**
Underdeveloped: (See Tilt-Factors list)

Commendable:

Overused:

Commitments
13. What do you want to honor for yourself and others in the arena? (See Commitments Guide)

Energizers and Accountability
14. My Energizers:

My Accountability Partner(s):

How I will show gratitude:

The Arena
15. What's my prize?
Example: *I reward myself for bravery regardless of outcome.*

RESOURCE PAGE

Course Title: *Empowerment Strategies*

sccLearn Resources
Bundles
- Empowering Employees

Additional Resources/Tools

Daring Greatly How the Courage to Be Vulnerable Transforms the Way We Live, Love, Parent, and Lead by Brené Brown

Every day we experience the uncertainty, risks, and emotional exposure that define what it means to be vulnerable, or to "dare greatly." Whether the arena is a new relationship, an important meeting, our creative process, or a difficult family conversation, we must find the courage to walk into vulnerability and engage with our whole hearts! In Daring Greatly, Dr. Brown challenges everything we think we know about vulnerability. Based on twelve years of research, she argues that vulnerability is not weakness, but rather our clearest path to courage, engagement, and meaningful connection.

Emotional Intelligence 2.0 by Travis Bradberry and Jean Greaves

In today's fast-paced world of competitive workplaces and turbulent economic conditions, each of us is searching for effective tools that can help us to manage, adapt, and strike out ahead of the pack. Emotional Intelligence 2.0 delivers a step-by-step program for increasing your EQ via four core EQ skills that enable you to achieve your fullest potential.

The Emotional Life of Your Brain by Richard J. Davidson

What is your emotional fingerprint? Why are some people so quick to recover from setbacks? Why are some so attuned to others that they seem psychic? Why are some people always up and others always down? In his thirty-year quest to answer these questions, pioneering neuroscientist Richard J. Davidson discovered that each of us has an Emotional Style, composed of Resilience, Outlook, Social Intuition, Self-Awareness, Sensitivity to Context, and Attention. Where we fall on these six continuums determines our own "emotional fingerprint." Sharing Dr. Davidson's fascinating case histories and experiments, The Emotional Life of Your Brain offers a new model for treating conditions like autism and depression as it empowers us all to better understand ourselves and live more meaningful lives.

Loving What Is by Byron Katie

Out of nowhere, like a breeze in a marketplace crowded with advice, comes Byron Katie and "The Work." The Work is simply four questions and turn-arounds that, when applied to a specific problem, enable you to see what is troubling you in an entirely different light. As Katie says, "It's not the problem that causes our suffering; it's our thinking about the problem." If you continue to do The Work, you may discover, as many people have, that the questioning flows into every aspect of your life, effortlessly undoing the stressful thoughts that keep you from experiencing peace.

Disclaimer: This resource page contains links to websites of organizations outside the County. While we offer these links for your convenience in accessing additional resources related to the topic discussed during the workshop, be aware that the policies that apply to their website may not be the same as the terms of use by the County. For more information, please go to the County of Santa Clara Links Policy.

Learning & Employee Development: https://learning.santaclaracounty.gov/home

sccLearn: http://scclearn.sccgov.org/

"Questioning our Fears and Beliefs, then intentionally planning for our Risk and Courage, will make our trip to the arena a success – no matter what."
--Simplified Coach

This work may not be copied, reproduced, or translated in whole or in part without prior and express written permission from Simplified Coach, Inc. Use with any form of information storage and retrieval, electronic adaptation, computer software, or by similar or dissimilar methods now known or developed in the future is strictly forbidden without prior and express written permission from Simplified Coach, Inc.

All rights reserved.

Copyright © 2024 Simplified Coach, Inc.   Version 3.0

Made in the USA
Columbia, SC
27 November 2024